Memories & Reflections Of Life in Guyana

By Norma Jean

Illustrated By Aislinn Papineau

Memories and Reflections of Life in Guyana
COPYRIGHT 2007 BY Norma Gangaram

All rights reserved. No part of this book may be used or reproduced in any manner whatsoever without written permission except in the case of brief quotation embodied in the critical articles and reviews.

Printed in Canada

Publisher Norma Gangaram

Registration No 1052246

ISBN 978-0-9780307-3-5

> **Dedicated to my Granddaughter, Taylor Ann**
> *My Taylor Rose*
> "Here are more of my childhood memories...
> ...written just for you"

This book belongs to: _____

Date: _____

If you borrowed this book and you enjoyed it, I invite you to purchase your own copy at http://www.childrensstories.ca

TABLE OF CONTENTS

Acknowledgements	2
Save the Bedding Fuh Me	4
Saturday in Guyana	14
Memories of Easter	26
The Chicken Under the Tin Cup	34
Bush Cook	42
Rickey Pounding the Foo Fu	50
Listen! The Masquerade is Coming	58
Saturday Night at the Sea Wall	66
The Bell Ringer	73
The Box Hand	80
Look Out 'Cane a Bun'	86
Sanitation Back Then	94
Wash Day	100
What Will I Feed the Baby?	108
About The Author	118

ACKNOWLEDGEMENTS

I would like to thank my husband for sharing some of his childhood stories with me over the years. At the time, I thought his stories were funny but I never thought I would write them for our granddaughter Taylor, whom we both simply adore.

I would like to thank my illustrator, Aislinn Papineau for the wonderful illustrations.

Also to Janice Byer, thank you for the wonderful set-up and layout of the book and the final editing.

Well done guys!

SAVE THE BEDDING FUH ME

When a young girl said to her neighbours, "please save some beddings fuh me," all the other women would know exactly what she meant. It meant she was pregnant and she was starting to prepare her nest for the new baby. Even in the wild every mother does some sort of preparation for the upcoming new arrival, her baby. Here is what I remember about a poor Guyanese woman making her preparation for her new baby.

Years ago, if a woman living in Guyana was having a baby, she had no idea what makes up a baby layette. A layette in North America meant setting up a nursery, which is a room for the baby filled with a new crib, dresser, change table, crib linen, new baby clothes that were ready-made and bought from the store, and lots of towels and disposable diapers. The linen would all match the curtains, wallpaper and decorations in the nursery. To the rich this all came so easily because there was usually enough money set aside for this purpose. Layette means a complete outfit for a new born baby including clothes, linen and all necessary accessories.

In a poor country like Guyana the word layette took on a brand new meaning. The expectant mother had a layette alright, but it was a poor mans layette because they would have to find creative ways of making this layette. Her layette would consist of hand sewn clothes for the new arrival, lots of cloth diapers made from new flour sacks, a handmade sweater, hat, booties, lots of bedding and in some cases a handmade crib. The handmade bonnets were so prettily trimmed with beautiful handmade crochet lace or sometimes contrasting trims of another fabric. There were also little smocked shirts for the baby to wear. In a lot of cases hand-me-down from other friends who did not need baby stuff any longer or on loan to be returned when the baby had out grown the clothes.

Miss Sybil had recently married and two months later she found out she was having a baby. At first she kept it quiet and would not tell anyone except her husband and mother. Sybil was very frightened, this was a brand new experience and she had no idea how to go about getting ready for the baby. The couple lived in a one room apartment. Everyday she was becoming a little heavier and some morning sickness was setting in.

Well it wasn't long into the pregnancy when she could no longer hide it. Sybil was having the worst morning sickness and she was beginning to get kind of heavy, she had been gaining weight in the middle of her belly. Sybil's next door neighbour noticed that she was not feeling very well and one day she saw her being sick and she suspected right away that a little one was on its way.

The word soon got around to the neighbourhood that the young bride was having a baby. All the women were excited for Sybil. A new baby is always welcome news in Guyana even if she already had a dozen children. You see in Guyana the people did not do family planning, they felt children were a blessing from God and he would be the one to decide when there should be no more children.

One weekend, Sybil and her husband John decided to visit her parents and spend the weekend with them. It's a time when Sybil's Mammie would give her lots of tender loving care. It's her mother's way of making sure that her daughter is eating right and getting the proper nutrition she needs.

While Mammie and her daughter were having some alone time together, she decided to talk to her daughter about her pregnancy, what to expect and what preparations she should be doing for the new baby. Sybil's mother was very conscious that her daughter knew nothing about having a baby and what might be involved, so she knew it was her job to coach her daughter as is the custom in Guyana. Sybil's Mammie remembered how scared she was when she had her first child.

Mammie made a list of the things Sybil needed to be doing to get ready:

1. Make a belly band
2. You need a rice jute bag to make a hammock with
3. Rope for hanging the hammock
4. Ask your neighbours to save you some bedding (used old clothing)
5. Start buying a lot of flour bags and bleach them. You will use these to make lots of diapers, bibs, and your belly band
6. You need to start making some white nighties and work the embroidery on them
7. Start buying some clothes for the baby
8. Make some bonnets for the baby for protection from the sun
9. Buy bottles and nipples
10. You will need lotion, cream, oil and Lifeboy soap
11. Make a straw bag for carrying the baby's supplies
12. Make lot of bibs and work some flower embroidery on it
13. Crocket a nice cotton shawl to wrap baby in
14. Buy towels and face clothes
15. Buy a big enamel basin to use for washing the baby

These were the most important items she would need to start with.

Returning home after the weekend, Sybil started to work on the list her Mom had made. Sybil thought, "me neva know me gat fuh do so much wuk." However, Sybil was feeling a little bit more confident about what she had to do to get ready for the new arrival. She knew that everything she had to do was time sensitive and had to follow the guide that her Mammie gave her. Sybil was quite shy about discussing her pregnancy and was very worried about how she would start to discuss the pregnancy with her older, wiser neighbours.

Monday morning Sybil called on her neighbours to ask them if they would save some 'bedding' for her. Many of the older ladies told Sybil that they had already started to save the beddings for her.

Then it was off to the grocery store to buy as much flour bags as she could get and to ask the grocer to save the bags for her because she was having a baby. Of course as soon as Sybil told the grocer that she needed the flour sacks the woman knew that a new baby was on the way and the grocer smiled and said, "don't worry child, I will take care of you!" The people were poor but they had a very silent code among the women when it came to being there for each other. The women had a sense of community and reached out without being asked. Sybil told the grocer that she would be back a couple times a week to check for the flour bags. Sybil did manage to secure six bags, so she went home and opened up the bags and soaked them in washing soda.

After soaking them, Sybil scrubbed the bags and put them out to bleach in the sun. This process was repeated until the bags were lily white.

Tuesday morning she decided it was time to do some sewing. Each bag was cut in four and the sides were hemmed. They are now looking like lily white diapers. Sybil made sixty diapers. All of a sudden Sybil was starting to be more confident that things would work out well, after all she had some very supportive women around her that were more than willing to take her under their wings and help guide her. Sybil smiled, "now what was I so afraid of? I have a wonderful extended family around me."

On Wednesday Sybil went to the fabric store and bought the best cotton she could afford. She went to one of her neighbours, who owned a sewing machine, to ask if she could use her sewing machine to sew some of the baby's shimmies. Shimmies is a term given to the little cotton night shirts that is worn by the baby.

The neighbour was very happy to help out any way she could. Neighbour Vivian, who was one of the elderly neighbours, was very experienced in sewing and also owned a sewing machine. Since she had twelve children of her own you can bet she knew what she was doing. She was a very good seamstress and made dresses and did lots of other sewing for others. Vivian helped Sybil cut out the shimmies and showed her how to do machine embroidery on the neckline. The shimmies took Sybil all month working at it a few hours everyday except weekends and they turned out beautiful. The shimmies had the mark of a mother's loving touch.

The neighbour, Vivian, showed Sybil how to make a belly band. These bands were used to tie around the belly to help the muscles to get toned again after the pregnancy. It helped her belly not to lose its elasticity and prevent her tummy from sagging. This band is usually worn everyday for three months

Next, it was time for the bonnets. Sybil used all the leftover cotton from the shimmies along with some ribbon and white lace. She also added some beautiful hand embroidery. They were darling little bonnets made with love. Any other piece of leftover fabric was used for making bibs. Every piece was then washed, starched, pressed and put in a drawer with moth balls.

Next Sybil started to crochet the most beautiful white cotton shawl to bring the baby home from the hospital. When the shawl was finished, it was a very intricate lacey pattern that was full of a mother's love and pride. It was fit for royalty.

Another neighbour lent Sybil a wood frame on which she wove a beautiful straw bag and then decorated it with some beautifully coloured flowers on the front of the bag.

The rest of the layette was bought from the nearby store and put on layaway. It was paid for a little each week as she could afford. Sybil also secured three large cardboard boxes in which the beddings would be packed.

Miss Sybil was making her final check one day to ensure she was ready for the new baby when she decided to give the bedding a final wash. As she pulled out the bedding from the box, all the next door neighbours could hear was this loud scream. They all thought something bad had happened to Miss Sybil so they ran to her rescue only to find out that Miss Sybil had two rats run out of the box. They looked in the box and there were about half a dozen newborn baby rats using her bedding before she could use it for her own baby.

The neighbours all laughed at her and one elderly neighbour chuckled, "we all thought you fell down and hurt yourself or went into labour, child." Two of the ladies then took the box outside and emptied it of all the bedding and its new residents and helped Sybil wash the beddings. The ladies, who were experienced mothers, had a good chuckle and reassured the young mother to be that this is what happens when you share your life with rodents. Vivian said to Sybil, "ten years from now you will also be laughing at the box of bedding and the rats."

The bedding would be used to make a bed for the baby to lie on and get changed every time the diaper was wet and needed to be changed. The baby slept in the middle of the bed between the parents. Dad on one side, baby in the middle and mom in the front of the bed because she had to get up so often throughout the night. Through the day the baby slept in the hammock filled with beddings for baby to lie on.

After the blessed event, all the neighbours were still laughing at the box of beddings and it residents. The poor rats were so confused they did not know what had happened to them that day.

I am sure that even today, this is how many poor families live and I felt it was worth writing about these struggles. The hardship did not hurt the babies in any way, shape or form. These babies have all grown up to be very successful men and women.

SATURDAY IN GUYANA

I was having a visit with one of my old friends from my school days and we started to reminisce about growing up and the entire buzz that went on Saturdays. As we stopped to reflect, we thought of all the joy and happiness the weekends brought and how much every child looked forward to the weekends. We were amazed at how much happened around us as children, which made Saturday very special to us.

Saturday was market day; all the farmers brought their produce to the local market. The market always happened in one key area. For example, the Diamond market happened on Saturdays in an area that the natives referred to as Billingate. Billingate was the entrance of the sugar factory. We made an interesting observation, that there was always a rum shop located near the Billingate and the market.

As we thought about this we realized that the owners made a mint from the rum shop. It was there because when the men received their pay, which was cold hard cash, they would stop in for a drink to celebrate the end of the week. This often led to their entire pay pocket spent on alcohol. As we talked, we remembered seeing and hearing of a lot of wives who would go to the factory and wait for their spouse's pay pocket, in order for them to have money to take care of the family for the week. It had to be so because if the men were left with the money, they over celebrated with their friends at the expense of the family.

Then we remembered the entrepreneur who would spend all day Friday making goodies to take to the market to sell. Miss Cooper made black pudding and souse. If you are Guyanese you sure know about black pudding and the mere sound of the name made your mouth water. Black pudding was made with rice, blood, seasoning and coconut milk, all cooked up and stuffed into a tripe casing, the round tubing or intestines of the cow that was carefully washed and prepared for this purpose. It was a very labour intensive job. A lot of lime juice was used in the preparation of the casing. When the casing was cleaned it looked white with absolutely no bad odour.

Then there was the souse with the fresh cucumber and hot pepper in it and you felt that crunch of the freshly picked cucumber under your teeth as you ate it. For a penny you could get a serving of black pudding and as you chowed down, you thought you had a real party going on in your mouth and you would savor every moment. The sight of a white enamel bucket with a cover brought back fond memories of that large coil of black pudding with the jar of mango sauce.

The souse was made from the skin on the face of the cow. It was roasted over a fire to burn all the tiny hairs from it. Then it would be scraped and boiled until it was tender. The water in the pot would be changed several times to get rid of all the thick gummy substance that came from the face. After the final change of water, a sauce made of lime juice, salt, onion and cucumber was served with the meat. This was usually sold by the roadside vendors on a Saturday evening.

Then there was Maa Mabel. She had a glass case loaded with Bara, Phoulourie made from ground split peas, flour, salt, herbs and deep fried Chana, which was chick peas boiled and fried, and the good old plantain chips were thinly sliced and fried to a crisp for munching on.

Next to her were a couple of white enamel buckets, one with mauby and the other with pineapple drink. You would be amazed at how far five cents could go. Mauby was a drink made from the bark of a tree native to the Caribbean. And the pineapple drink was made from the skin of the pineapple.

A little ways down, there was Auntie Cecelia, and in her glass case she had buns, Salara, pineapple tarts, cassava pone, and fried fish and bread with lots and lots of pepper sauce. We remember the joy of buying fried fish and bread with a glass of mauby to wash it down and a piece of cassava pone or a pineapple tart to cool off our tongues.

The buns were bread made with flour, sugar, margarine and a generous amount of grated coconut. They were baked in a mud oven over hot coals. The pineapple was a pastry filled with pineapple filling made much like jam. Salara was bread dough filled like a jelly roll, only the filling would be toasted coconut, sugar, essence and red food colouring baked in the oven. The cassava pone was made of grated cassava, which is a root vegetable, lots of grated coconut, sugar, raisins and vanilla baked in the oven to a golden brown crust on top.

Then there was Miss Vanessa with her glass case packed full of Donkey collar, Salara, coconut rolls, buns, tennis rolls, sugar cakes with a choice of grated or chipped coconut, crow crow, jellabee and potato balls. These were all desserts that are native to Guyana.

If you wished you could always go to the local cake shops that were well stocked for the weekend. At the shop you could get a pint of local wine poured from a barrel, Mauby, tennis rolls and cheese, lemonade and cheese rolls. The large glass case would be loaded with fresh bread of every size; five, ten or twenty-five cent loaves. The twenty-five cent loaf was big enough for a family of five.

Back at the market there would be the women carrying their bags or baskets to take home their purchases. The women would buy everything they would need to cook for the next week. Some of the items were vegetable, root vegetables, fresh fish, shrimp and crabs and as they walked home they would stop at the local butcher to buy some beef or pork.

I also recall my mother waking up early to set the yeast to make bread and this would be quite a production. She would knead her bread in a large aluminum bowl designed to make bread and salara. By two in the afternoon, the flour would have risen and ready to bake. She would them get two large cookie sheets on which she would put the bread and the salara for baking. The price to bake the bread was twenty-five cents per sheet. It would be my job to take the dough to the bakery, taking one sheet at a time. Mr. Sobers would tell me what time to return for the bread, usually he would say, "come back in one hour child", and I would go home.

The bakery would always be full of people, all laughing and chatting, waiting to have their bread baked. For some of the patrons, it was a social time and also a time to catch up with the gossip of the village. Often times the bakery would have lots of men from the neighbourhood and, as I recall, I never felt nervous, scared or threatened of any anyone harming me. As a matter of fact, they all looked out for me. They were all like father figures, very caring. I would guess that they would have gone to any lengths to protect me. When I returned to collect the bread, I would bring my basket and tea towel, which was white and made from a bleached flour sac, to cover my bread for the walk home. I covered the basket of bread, making sure the beautiful hand embroidery was on the top for presentation purposes.

Often there would be someone whose bread was finished baking and there would be butter on the counter, I mean real butter, and you would be welcome to have some fresh baked bread. The smell would make your mouth water and all your senses would be filled with nothing but fresh baked bread.

I must pause here to tell you about Mr. Sobers. First of all, Mr. Sobers was a man who had lost both of his legs. He wore a leather Knee shoe which looked like a cup on each knee. He walked on it as though it were his feet in shoes. He was an incredible man. He owned a little wood shack and in the shack was a big oven made of bricks and fired by wood and coal.

It always amazed me how the men that worked the oven knew when it was the right temperature.

On Saturday afternoons, Mr. Sobers would get on his cart with his donkey. The cart would be loaded with all kinds of baked goods. Mr. Sobers would take a comfortable seat on a box and go around the village to sell his fresh baked bread and desserts. That was how Mr. Sobers made his living, even though he had no feet. That did not stop the man from being successful and earning a decent living.

Then there was another neighbour on her donkey cart, Miss Early. She sold rice, paddy, coconut oil and cooking oil. We remember knowing when she was on her way because you would hear, "oil, oil, paddy and rice!" Miss Early would repeat this chant over and over and the village people would come out of their homes to meet Miss Early at the cart to make their purchases. Paddy is the original rice pod before the husk was removed and this is what the fowls and ducks would be fed.

I must tell you about the coconut oil; this oil was such versatile oil. Every mother used it in their childrens' hair and it was their all-time favorite moisturizing lotion. After a bath, the mothers would lather the coconut oil on the body. It helps stop the sun from drying out the natural oils of the body. We remembered how shiny our skin looked and healthy.

Then there was the lovable Miss Ena and Mr. Dean. Miss Ena and Mr. Dean were the local fishmongers. These two people would credit their fish and shrimp to the local people who had no money and would come around to collect on Saturdays. I remember my mother parceling out her money on a shelf, noting who got what just in case she was not around when they came. This was her way of paying her debt and fulfilling her obligations. It was an amazing system all based on just plain old pure trust.

As we looked back we could not get over the trust and honesty that existed among everyone. It seemed to us that just about everyone was totally trustworthy. It was a period when just about anything could be had even if you did not have money; they all made sure no one went without. These vendors knew that Friday or Saturday they would be paid. Even though there were poor, mean and lean times, no one worried about tomorrow. Now that I am all grown up, I am surer than ever, there was so much love there; one had to live it to understand that love.

Saturdays were also wash days. All the school uniforms were washed, starched and pressed making them ready for Monday morning. The yachting shoes were all scrubbed with a coconut brush and put to dry. After they were dry they were whitened with powder dissolved in a little water and applied to the yachting. Even the laces were spotless. All the hair ribbons were washed and pressed for reusing the following week.

Saturday was also cleaning day. It was a time when all the children were home and they all had to pitch in and help with the cleaning. Our mothers would delegate the chores and we would have no choice but to do as we were told. If we didn't we would get such a licking we would never forget it. My mother would say, "you do as me tell or you can give God you soul and give me you backside."

Saturday was also the busiest day in the city. Some people would go by bus to the city to do their shopping and special purchases.

We remembered the smell of ripe fruits as you disembark the bus, and hearing the loud sound of voices, everyone trying to talk at the same time. As a child you looked forward to such a trip because it only came a few times a year and it was a special treat, like an ice-cream cone. I loved the hustle and bustle, talking and laughter yet everyone minding their own business as if they were on a mission.

Oh Saturday afternoon! Saturday afternoons had a totally different kind of buzz. Mothers picking up the laundry from the outdoor clothesline, most of the laundry stiffly starched. The laundry is then made ready for ironing by being sprinkled with water and put in a basket to moisten (giff). The kitchen is also busy with mothers making a special dinner, usually the once a week meal of meat and a special dessert. In Guyana, in those days, no one ate dessert with their meals, it was not affordable. Dessert was considered a special treat; the family would all have a meal together. All the children were given a pocket piece (allowance).

After all the chores were done, everyone took a shower and dressed in some fine Saturday clothes. After supper some of the boys would go to the movies and the girls would do some ironing and sewing and take it easy.

When it started to get dark, dotted along the way were vendors and little stands with lanterns to see in the dark. The vendors would sell bara, phulories, aloo ball and channa. Another vendor selling souse and black pudding and yet another selling cakes like pine tarts, salara, cassava pone, cheese roll, coconut roll, tennis roll and touwsa (back bean cake).

The movie-goers would buy their snack of choice and take it into the movies along with a big bottle of coke. We knew every vendor and we certainly knew who had our favorite snacks. For me the best snack, after the black pudding, was the hot roasted peanuts.

Uncle Albert had a cut-off oil drum with a big Karahi (wok) on it with sand and the peanuts would be roasting on the open fire. Uncle Albert kept turning the sand for an even roast. Imagine for six cents you could have a pound of roasted peanuts.

It seems like I have so much to say and yet I have not told you about the radio, which many called the wireless. We had no television, just a short wave radio with two radio stations… Radio Demarara and Guyana broadcasting service. Saturday evenings would be an all request program for birthdays and special requests. We would have the radio at top volume and would sing along with the music. I was very lucky, we had a Telefunkin radiogram and we would just blast the Jim Reeves music and friends would drop in to have a chat and enjoy the music.

As it got later into the evening we would sometimes get hungry and my father would splurge and send us to the corner cake shop to buy some fresh baked bread and a can of corned beef and cheese, a pint of red wine, some cream soda and a tin of carnation milk. And as a special treat from our pocket piece we would buy some hassaback and coconut biscuits.

My family was lucky because my dad worked at the local sugar factory and on the side he did some tailoring at home for other people. Once in a while, as a special treat, the family took a bus into the city. This happened only once a year when my father got his "one for all bonus" which I believe was profit sharing for the sugar worker. My dad would take us to Brown Betty for supper (chicken in the rough) and chips served in a basket and dessert would be an ice cream cone. Even today, I have not tasted any ice cream so good. I guess the ice cream was made of nothing but whole milk.

Well, I think by now you've got the picture. My point is even though we were dirt poor, we were quite content and happy. The truth is, we did not know any other way of life and you know the old saying, "you cannot miss what you have never had." I cannot help thinking of Guyana. Even though it is a small country, it is a country so very rich in culture, unique only to Guyana.

MEMORIES OF EASTER

Reflecting on my childhood and all the wonderful memories, I just had to write about them for my granddaughter and all the other children of Canadian-Guyanese parents and grandparents out there who will never experience those days. I thought the next best way for others to have that experience is to read about it. I hope it helps my granddaughter to have a better understanding of how to some extent my background has influenced my life and hers. It all starts with the Easter curtains, in Easter colours, being hung on the windows on Thursday evening.

Growing up in a very multicultural society like Guyana where everyone showed respect for the other persons and their religious beliefs, I did not understand prejudice until I was much older. Good Friday was a day when most Guyanese ate vegetarian meals; you would be hard pressed to find a home that had cooked meat on that day. I guess it was in respect for the day and what it meant and in respect for others also.

On Good Friday all the Christians went to church dressed in black or dark mourning colours. They were mourning the fact that Jesus was crucified on that day; even non-Christians honored the day's dress code. Not much else went on that day except church services. Even on the air waves or wireless one can sense the solemness. None of the stores were open and all work places were shut down in respect for the holiday.

During the week leading up to Easter, the fabric stores would be most busy and business was great. The stores would be well stocked with rich colourful fabrics. If you needed to purchase some fabric you would have to wait in a long line to get it measured and cut. People would be buying fabric to make new Easter outfits like dresses, shirts, pants and new curtains for the window dressings. It was one of the peak times for tailors and seamstresses, all having deadlines for their orders.

Yet there were many who were lucky enough to own a sewing machine and they would attempt to make their own outfits. There were a few stores with ready-made clothing. If ready-made clothing was available, the cost of it would be out of reach financially for the average Guyanese. Only the very privileged would be able to afford such luxury.

At home, all the walls were washed and the windows gleaming. The house would get a very thorough spring cleaning. Everything that can shine was polished, such as the brassware, stove, polished floors and yes, even the buckets, which were made of galvanized steel would shine when scrubbed. The floors! Oh the floors; they were polished with dark mansion wax polish and then buffed to a shine that dazzled the eyes. By the end of the day Thursday, all the chores would be finished and Good Friday was very solemnly observed with the greatest respect.

I remember waking up to religious music on the air waves. My mother would wake up before the family and start to prepare our breakfast. We were greeted with a meatless breakfast. There would be hot cross buns and cheese, and no one even thought of complaining. We knew that is just the way it was. After breakfast we would all have our shower and get dressed for church at 10:00 am. My brothers in black dress pants and white shirts, my sister and I in black and white also and off we went to church with our mother. There was no complaining, we kids just did as we were told.

Lunch would be all homemade goodies, Bara, Phoulori and Aloo ball filled with potatoes, a meatless meal made of ground split peas and flour with spicy hot mango sauce. Then there was Channa, which was made of chick peas. For desert, it would be rice pudding with lots of raisin and cherries. After lunch everyone would be doing their own thing to get ready for the weekend.

For supper that day Mom made Roti and curried potatoes with a vegetable like Bora (long bean), Bigan (eggplant), Squash or whatever vegetable was available and in season. My favorite vegetable was roasted eggplant (Bigan) which was seasoned with onion, salt, green onion and vegetable oil, eaten with a hot Roti. It was so good it was like having a party in my mouth with all my taste buds dancing a jig. No one even dreamt of mentioning the word alcohol, it was unthinkable. It would be sacrilegious and it would be regarded as downright sinful. It was a quiet and reflective day respected by all.

We have now arrived at Saturday and it was a busy day in Guyana. The pace of Saturday was certainly different from the quiet Good Friday. Mother checked on her ginger beer, which was made of ground ginger that sat in the sun in a large jar for about one week, and Mauby. The Mauby was made from the bark of a tree native to the Caribbean. Then she would mix the bread dough for her bread and her hot cross buns. The oldest child was given the job of grating the cassava and the coconut for the cassava pone, while another washed the salt out of the butter to make the butter sponge cake. All necessary shopping would have been done. Only a little bit of laundry would be done on that day, just the school uniforms as we had only one set.

Some people would pick up their new outfit from the tailors and seamstresses. Added to all the special cooking there would still be the mundane chores to be done. Mother would make a fish supper, likely stewed or curried fish with rice and a cucumber salad. Sunday would be the day that a meat meal would be prepared. The boys would all be busy working on their colourful kites until late into the evening. All the kites were homemade with wood frames and covered with colourful tissue.

The day everyone looked forward to was Sunday. Oh Sunday! What a day! For me Sunday was so special. When I think of Easter Sunday I think of colour, colour, and more colour!

For church on Sunday morning everyone would be dressed in a new dress and there would be the most beautiful kaleidoscope of colours among the women's hats and dresses. Black, white and navy blues were reserved for Good Friday and funerals while red and white were for Christmas. For Easter, all the other bright pastels were worn. The warmth of the colours gave me a warm fuzzy feeling inside, and my heart felt like it was singing. My most favorite Easter dress was the year my sister and I wore beautiful bright peach frocks. Even today I still love a bright peach colour.

The significance of the kite in Guyana has to do with the fact that Christ rose on the third day. Everyone participated, Christians and non-Christian alike. By 2:00 p.m. the skies would be filled with kites, colourful kites of all sizes and shape and the beautiful hum that resonated from the flying kites. Every child took part in the sport, rich or poor, and every parent helped, coached or guided their child or children in the art of flying their kites. In the evening it was very difficult to get everyone to come in for supper. No one wanted to leave their kites.

Easter Monday was also a holiday and the celebrating continued. Monday was a more laid back kind of day where everyone was busy flying their kites. However mother made another delicious meal using all of the leftovers from the past three days. It seemed like all I did on Monday was snack, snack and snack. I guess it's not hard to tell we all loved our food.

One of my most memorable acts was that of the neighbours sharing their baked goodies and special dishes with each other. My mother would make little packages and send us off to the different neighbours. Mother said it was to give them a sample of her goodies but quietly we all knew it was to make sure that no one went without during the holidays. It was also another way of making sure that everyone had some treats. The meal times were an open table where anyone who dropped in was welcome. No one went without food on that day, not even the panhandlers.

These are a few of my memories of Easter. I wrote this for my granddaughter who may never experience this joy and happiness. I also wanted her to know how important our community was and how important reaching out was in a poor community.

Guyana is truly a multicultural country. Everyone respects each other's religions and joined in the celebration. I consider myself very lucky to have never experienced prejudice growing up as a child.

THE CHICKEN UNDER THE TIN CUP

If I told my granddaughter that I resuscitated chickens and ducklings when I was young, I am sure she would laugh and say, "Grandma is just fooling."

It was Sunday morning and I was holding an empty coffee tin in my hand. Without any warning my head started to fill with memories of the chicken in the backyard under the five pound golden cream margarine tin. I recall my brother and I beating the heck out of that tin with the chicken under it. Well now that I have said that, I guess I will tell you about the fate of this chicken.

Most home-owners in Guyana, regardless of where they lived, had a fowl pen in their yard (chicken coupe). Everyone raised their own chickens and ducks for their meat consumption. There was a large number of Guyanese who do not eat beef or pork for religious reasons. The Hindu's do not eat beef or pork and the Muslims do not eat any pork. It is a good thing our country is so blessed with an abundance of seafood. Seafood and poultry was the most popular choice of protein as well as the eggs from the poultry. Special occasion meat was goat or sheep.

My mother's fowl pen had at least forty chickens, young and old. These chickens were very intelligent, they knew where their pen was and in the pen were ladders that they all perched on to sleep. They all headed to the pen at about 6p.m. to retire for the night and they all knew who sat where on the ladders. The other half of the pen was for the ducks and they also manifested the same pattern of behavior at nightfall.

In the pen were nesting boxes for the chickens and ducks. It seemed as though there were always some chickens and ducks hatching or laying their eggs at any given time. The hens would pick a nesting box and would stick to it for the duration of twenty-one days. Each and every day of the week, the eggs laid in the nesting boxes would be collected in the afternoon and taken into the kitchen. After a few weeks of laying their eggs the hens would stay in their box all day and would cackle all day, which was an indication that the hens were ready to hatch a new set of chicks.

The hen's box would then be cleaned and freshened up with clean straw and the eggs, usually never more than one dozen, would be set in the clean nest for the hen. The hen would then retire to the nest for the next three weeks, leaving only for short periods each day to feed and to drink water. After three weeks the eggs would start hatching. The mother hen would pick at the eggshell to help the chick to leave the shell. One by one she would repeat the same process until all the chicks were hatched. Mother hen would bring food in her mouth to the nest to feed the chicks. The hens would eat and fill their craw and then they would regurgitate the food into the baby's mouth. As soon as the chickens are strong enough, the mother hen would lead them out of the nest and introduce them to their living environment.

These new chicks were the pride and joy of my mother. They were fed twice a day, once when they were let out in the morning from the pen and again in the evening just before they retired for the night.

They were carefully checked and counted to make sure the mongoose or snake did not eat any chicks. They were fed paddy, which is the rice before the husk is removed. The ducks were fed in a large galvanized pan a diet of rice husk (boosee) and water. The ducks were also counted to make sure none were missing.

None of the feed was processed food. It was all natural grains and husks. The rice husk was given free, to anyone who wanted it, from the local rice factory. As I previously mentioned, we lived in a very co-operative community and everyone looked out for each other. It certainly was not all about money, in spite of the fact that everyone was dirt poor. The ducks, drakes, ducklings, hens, roosters and chicks were allowed to run free all day. I guess we were eating free run chickens for more years than I can remember.

Those livestock were regarded as part of the family; it would be a cardinal sin to hurt any of those chickens. Mother would be working in the kitchen and the chickens would come in and run around between her feet. They just came and went as they pleased. Each and every day, as the children went out to play, they would be given the same warning by my mother, "children, look out for the chicks and ducklings! You hear me?"

Well, getting back to the newly hatched chicks, just after we were given the warnings, guess what? My brothers and their friends were playing in the backyard and yes, one of the boys did step on one of the new chicks. My younger brother hollered, "oh gawd, we in big, big trouble now! Mammie gon be mad, mad, mad with us!" Just then someone yelled, "get a tin cup, one big enough to put over the chick." All I could find was an empty five pound golden cream margarine container, so I grabbed it and gave it to the boys. One of the boys put the chick under the tin cup and with a small twig they started to hit the bottom of the tin which was upside down as if it were a musical drum.

After a few minutes, the boys lifted the tin can and the chick ran away as if nothing was the matter. The chick was well and perky and ran to his mommy. We all stood there in amazement, breathing a sigh of relief that we would not have to tell Mammie about the ill fate of a chick. I guess you could call it backyard shock treatment. Living in a poor country, we knew nothing about veterinarians and people invented their own treatment. My older brother said, "hush everyone; no one is to mention a word about this."

The game continued as if nothing happened; well wouldn't you know one of the other boys stepped on a little duckling. The duckling was lying there stunned and lifeless with a faint cry. We all could hear my mother's words, "wah miss you na pass you!" Yes the boys got the margarine tin out again and tried to perform magic again. They quickly stuck the duckling under the tin and two of the boys started to hit the tin again. After a few minutes the boys lifted the tin and the duckling was still a bit stunned, so the two boys continued to beat the drum in rhythms which almost sounded like music. Everyone looked on and hoped for the duckling to live. If Mammie lost one of her ducklings she would not take kindly to that. Finally they lifted the tin and the duckling ran out as if she had seen a ghost, never looking back. She ran to the safety of mom. My guess is she was glad to run from the deafening sound of the tin.

The problem that day was our mother was away and she had given the charge to my brother and I to take care of things while she was away. My older brother okayed the cricket game in the backyard for the younger boys and my baby sister, who was standing there, tattled, "I gon tell Mammie you kill the duckling and the chicken."

My brother and I had no idea who my mom would blame for the mishap since we were both supposed to be in charge. Oh how we prayed that chick and duckling would stay alive. Both the chick and the duckling lived to be adults and I am sure glad we never had to perform that exercise again.

This was the memory that a coffee tin evoked in me. You see mom can handle a mongoose eating one of her chickens but she had no tolerance for any of us kids hurting her pride and joy.

BUSH COOK

In Guyana, all Guyanese believe that there is no food cooked that is a sweet as a bush cook. I have pondered this statement many times and the only answer I can think of is, 'a taste of the forbidden, when you can get away with it, always feels good because of the satisfaction that you have beaten the system'.

On a well lit moonlit night, usually a Friday night, it seemed as if a lot of young men got up to all sorts of mischief. Groups of young men in the neighbourhood usually got together for a gaff, a game of dominoes and a game of cards called chupchal. The games would go well, so well in fact that they would lose track of time.

One Friday evening, as it was getting well in to the night, in fact into the early morning hours, the boys were starting to get hungry. Of course, none of the stores or restaurants were open. So the boys all agreed to make "a bush cook". They agreed on what each one would contribute towards the cook. So off some of the boys went to fetch their donation towards the meal.

Some of the boys lit a fire on the sea dam and put on a big pot of water to boil. Horace said, "boys, it would sure be nice if we had a chicken fowl", and all the boys looked at each other with a down right mischievous look in their eyes. It was as if you could see the wheels were turning in their heads. They all seemed to know what each other were thinking. With a grin on his face, Jerry blurted, "Auntie Moon. What do you say boys?" With one big chuckle, Jerry announced, "come on buddies, we have a job to do that can only flava this bush cook."

I should remind you the folks in Guyana raised their own poultry for eggs and meat for food consumption in their very own backyards. Not very many of the natives ate beef and pork, therefore poultry was the choice of protein. Every home had a fowl pen (henhouse). At night the chickens and ducks seemed to instinctively know where their beds were for the night and one by one they would retire to the fowl pen (henhouse). In the morning, the chickens and ducks would all come out of the pens and walk around in the yard. The only ones left in the pen were the hens that were sitting on their eggs waiting to hatch. Well Auntie Moon was one of those folks with quite a full pen of poultry.

So the boys cooked up a plan and armed themselves with a wet rice bag (Jute bag big enough to hold one hundred gallons of rice. In my childhood days the measurement used was the imperial method). The boys quietly made their way to Auntie Moon's backyard fowl pen. They quietly opened the fowl pen door making sure they did not disturb the dogs. However, the dogs heard the boys and started to bark. The boys thought that was a good thing because the barking would drown out the noise of the chickens cackling, but it would also mean they would have to move as fast as they could and get out of the yard before Auntie Moon and her family was alarmed by the dogs' loud barking.

So the boys took the wet rice sac and threw it over the chickens to muffle the noise. They grabbed the first chicken they could lay their hands on and made a fast exit. The idea was to take what you can get, one, only one chicken and leave. After all, all they needed for the pot was one chicken for 'flava for the bush cook.'

Well wouldn't you know, the boys grabbed Auntie Moon's oldest hen that was sitting in the pen on one dozen eggs. Jerry gave the hen to the main cook, Jeff. Jeff was an excellent cook, so along with Floyd and Horace, it took no time at all for the chicken to be prepared and immersed in the boiling water. The boys were not sure they were able to remove all the fine feathers so they roasted the outer skin to burn all the feathers off.

Horace, who was very skillful at using a cutlass (machete), was responsible for cutting wood for the fire and was given the job of sectioning the chicken and cutting it in small pieces.

The iron skillet pot was put back on the fire and the chicken was put in to brown, I mean really brown, then the water was added and brought to a boil. In went the rice salt, split peas, seasoning, some chopped cassava, plantain, onion, some hot pepper, which the boys called hot scenting peppa, and a can of carnation milk.

Over a slow heat of red hot coals the food was slowly cooked for about one hour or more. By the time all the ingredients were well cooked and married in with the flavors, the rice was soft and the boys knew the food was finished. By 3:30 am, in the dark of night lit only by moonlight and a jug lantern, the boys sat down to a bush cook. The hot meal was very quickly cooled by the cool fresh night air.

As Horace sat down on the edge of the dam to eat, he picked up a piece of chicken and bit down on the meat, Horace bawled, "Oh Gawd this fowl prapa hard, me can't even bite down on the meat. Ee like old leather, this meat ah bite me back man", and everyone burst out with a great big laughter. Allan scolded Horace, "listen here, the fowl flava the food, just shut you mouth up and eat you food." Just then Jerry blurted, I bet al' you tek Auntie Moon oldest hen or she setting fowl, you know setting fowl na good fuh eat." This was a horrible thought and the boys all laughed and hoped that they did not steal a setting fowl. The boys had their meal and laughed and talked until almost sunset and, as the sun started to come up, the boys all went home.

The next morning, at about eight o'clock, Auntie Moon could be heard in her yard saying, "somebody thief me setting hen last night and now all me eggs gan spoil. I hope whoever tek me hen get good and sick fuh eating setting fowl, dam thief man, God ga sin them fuh disturbing a setting fowl. That is just like eating a pregnant animal... what a sin!"

Word soon spread to the boys and the boys enjoyed another hearty laugh knowing full well they did steal Auntie Moon's setting fowl. As the story was being related to the boys, they could not stop laughing. What the person telling the story did not know was that he was speaking to the perpetrators.

So the storyteller asked the boys, "how come you enjoy this story so much, like you know something?"

This was a typical bush cook, if you are a Guyanese man you are bound to know about a bush cook and how it is done. It is a bit of everything you can lay your hands on from your Mamma's kitchen except the setting hen. To young men growing up, this is part of the culture, and at some point and time in every young man's life, they would be involved in a bush cook. This all makes up part of Guyana's culture. This practice was also done by the men working in the cane fields on a Friday. It was like a celebration for the end of a week, the same meal enjoyed by all and I guess it was a sort of picnic.

RICKEY POUNDING THE FOO FU

Every Guyanese can relate to having a meal of Foo Fu. If you haven' eaten Foo Fu, you are not a real Guyanese. I am not sure why this meal is so loved, maybe because it is such a labour intensive meal to prepare. By the time the meal is cooked you are starving.

It was almost month's end and it was a time when everything in the grocery cupboard was running low. This would be so if you got paid monthly, of course. Well Miss Thelma was no different than any other of the natives, her husband got paid monthly. Miss Thelma looked in the cupboard and it was bare, so she cried out loud, "Lordie! Lordie! What will I feed my family today? Only God gon have to provide something fuh me today!" Miss Thelma had a quiet thought and with that thought in mind she left the house as she hollered out to Rickey, "Rickey, keep an eye on the house. I going up the street and I will soon come back." "Okay Mammie", he assured his mother distractedly as he continued his game of marbles with his friends, especially since it was his turn to chink. The object of the game marbles is to get you marble into the hole with the skill and accuracy of your hand, sort of a mini golf game without the clubs.

Miss Thelma went down the street to pay Mr. Khan a visit. Mr. Khan was the local village butcher. The butcher is usually a Muslim because the meat has to be halal (blessed) before the slaughter. Mr. Khan was a very kind man and made it his business to know his customers very well and, in this culture, everything was done on a trust system. When he saw Thelma coming to the shop and he knew it was month's end and her cupboard must be empty. So, without a word being said, Mr. Khan knew what he had to do. "Good morning, Mr. Khan! How you doing boy?" Mr. Khan replied "Good morning, Thelma! I was just thinking of you and I put some soup bones aside fuh you."

"Oh Gawd boy, you don't know how me gad fuh this bone here boy. Is month end, you know things are pretty brown", exclaimed Miss Thelma. Mr. Khan, being a very kind man told Thelma, "you don't have to explain to me gal, me understand you plight too well." And with that he packaged the bones, making sure there was some meat on the bones, and handed it to Miss Thelma.

Back at home Miss Thelma put on a big pot of water to boil to make some soup. Thelma added the beef bones and then some peas and left the pot on the fireside to boil slowly; while that was cooking she went down the street to her neighbour Malinda. Miss Malinda had lots of plantain suckers in her yard and some were bearing huge bunches of plantains ready for picking. Among the villagers, there was a silent code of reaching out and helping whenever they could or whenever the opportunity presented itself. This code allowed the person in need to keep his or her dignity. One thing you can be sure of, there are no questions or probing in the person's personal life for private information.

Miss Thelma greeted Malinda, "good morning! How are you gal?"

"Good morning, Thelma gal! What you up to this fine morning?" chuckled Malinda as she greeted Thelma. Miss Thelma explained to Malinda, "gal you know is month end and you know how it is".

Miss Malinda mumbled, "Hmmmm, I know gal you don't have to tell me. Wah you need Thellie gal? Tell me nah!" Melinda asked of Thelma. "Could give me some plantains?" Without any hesitation Malinda went to her storeroom and retrieved some plantains, cassava and eddoes, placed them in a bag and handed it to Thelma. Miss Thelma was so grateful for the offering and visited with Malinda for about half hour then left for home to check on the soup that was slowly boiling on the fireside.

Back in her kitchen, Miss Thelma decided to use the plantain to make some foo fu to eat with the soup. Outside in their yard, Rickey was very involved in his game of marbles when he heard his mother call for him to come in the house, she needed his help. "Rickey, Rickey come hay boy, me need you to pound this plantains." Rickey heard his mother but he was so involved in his game he pretended not to hear her calls. Rickey hoped that she would give up and do the job herself. Miss

Thelma went back in the house to clean the mortar and pestles for pounding the plantains.

Rickey continued to ignore his mother, not wanting to go into the house to help or leave his friends and the game.

All of a sudden Rickey heard, "Rickey, you come in hay right now or you will have no backside to sit on! I need you the very minute, you hear me boy?" Well that was enough to grab Rickey's attention and he hollered, "a coming Mammie, a coming Mammie!"

Pounding the plantain was a very labour intensive job and it was usually given to the oldest child or the strongest male child, that is, if there were any children in the home. This freed the mother up to do other chores. So Rickey washed his hands and took his seat on a small bench in front of the mortar. The plantain was cooked and given to Rickey. He started pounding, pounding, pounding and pounding. Two hours later Rickey was finished pounding, his mother finally approved the texture of the plantain and deemed it ready to be made into foo fu.

In the meantime, Thelma was checking on the soup and seasoning it just right. Thelma then made her plantain into small round balls the size of a golden apple and they were added to the soup. The aroma of the soup filled the kitchen making Rickey very hungry. After all, he exerted a lot of energy getting those plantains ready. As his Mammie was busy cooking, Rickey washed and cleaned the mortar and pestles and stored it in its corner of the kitchen

Finally the soup was ready and Thelma smiled and said, "thank you Lord for providing for us another day even when it seems like there would be none." The family enjoyed a hearty meal of foo fu soup and was all satisfied and full.

If you are a Guyanese you've got to know about our famous Foo fu soup. The idea of this meal was brought from Africa by the slaves and today it is enjoyed as one of our national cuisines. There is nothing more comforting than a hot bowl of Foo fu soup.

LISTEN! THE MASQUERADE IS COMING

In Guyana, every child can relate to the excitement of hearing the sounds of distant drums and I was no exception. The sound of these drums drew every child toward the road to view this colourful spectacle.

It was the Christmas season and the sounds of drums in the distance could be heard. This was a sound that was enough to get all the children excited and start running towards the main road to see the colourful costumes, dancers and the people in the bands with their painted faces. The beat of the bongo could be heard from about a mile away and the children were drawn to it like metal to a magnet.

The culture of the masquerade was brought to Guyana by the African slaves. It was a part of African culture somewhere in West Africa. It was truly wonderful to watch Guyanese come together and celebrate with diverse colours, the true spirit of unity. The masquerade to me also represented the love and hospitality of Guyana and I like to think of my country as people of togetherness.

The masquerade is the oldest practicing art form of our land. Some of the masquerades represented were the flounce, mother Sally, the mad bull, plus there were many other images that were very colourful and are still as fresh as ever in my mind. The most memorable memory was the acrobatic dancers, a sure reminder of our African heritage.

You would be hard pressed to be able to stand in one spot to watch a masquerade parade. It seemed like your body just automatically imitated the movement of the masquerade dancers which was so contagious in nature. Before you knew it you were shaking your bootie.

In my mind the masquerade at Christmas seemed to bridge all cultures and it was a joy to see people laughing and embracing each other in a dance or two. If only for a moment the masquerade seemed to conquer racism and transform people. It seemed to refresh the people like a limacol freshness.

The masquerade was and is as Guyanese as black pudding, souse, the kissing bridge in the botanical gardens and our sea wall. It is the bridge that bridges the gap between toddlers, teenagers, parents and grandparents. I believe that because this parade takes place at the end of the year it seemed like the final glue in the puzzle that binds its people together for all times.

During the Christmas season, the masquerade on our streets had become part of our culture and heritage. The puppets on a long pole, fondly known as the "long lady", would be the face of a woman dressed in a very colourful long, long dress. She would be about twenty or twenty five feet tall, dressed in a colourful frock, an African cotton head tie, a wooden beaded necklace and bright big earrings. She would be held up high by one of the band members.

Others would be carrying different puppets such as a donkey, a cow, a monkey, and an overgrown rooster all held up in the air on poles and the way they were moved they seemed to be dancing as the person holding them dances. Of course the face masks were very artfully designed, it was hard to tell who was wearing it. It took months of planning to make this masquerade parade possible. Yet as a child it all seemed very simple and uncomplicated, as seen through the childrens' young innocent eyes.

The drums and bongos would be beating to the tune of Christmas carols and everyone, young and old, sang the tunes of the carolers.

The colourful masked men would enter each and every yard and dance for the folks and in turn would be given a monetary offering for their entertainment.

As a child I could not understand why the masqueraders wanted money but as I got older I now realized that the money collected helped to offset the cost of putting on such a parade. The masqueraders did not make any profit; the parade was done for entertainment and the love of doing so by the men of the band. It was sharing the spirit of Christmas. Had it not been for love, why else would anyone want to walk and dance for eight or nine hours with the hot sun bearing down on them. The masqueraders danced from one village to another and the children would scream with excitement and join in the celebration. You know what they say, "happiness is contagious". Well, it definitely spread to the adults; it seemed to get the adults into the Christmas spirit.

This masquerading went on for two weeks, one week before Christmas and the week between Christmas and New Year.

As the masqueraders danced from village to village it would be very evident how the joy just spread to young and old. This culture was brought to Guyana by the African slaves that came from Ghana. The masquerade is still alive and well in our culture at Christmas in Guyana.

I remember as a child one Christmas season, I was washing the salt out of some butter for my mother. The idea was to take as much salt as possible out of the butter in order to make a perfect butter sponge cake. My mother was multi-tasking in the kitchen with so much to be done in preparation for Christmas.

My friend Chandra came to the door and said to me, "come, come, come lets go see the long lady masquerade, it coming down the road, I can see the long lady!" Well wouldn't you know it, with total disrespect for the task given to me, I dropped the spoon in the butter and without saying a word to my mother I took off with my friend for the main road. You see when the masquerade is coming everything stops, yes even the traffic. The sides of the road were lined with people big and small and as the masquerade drew closer you could feel the excitement in the air building and building.

My friend and I joined in the festivities and we were dancing to the beat of the drums. For a brief moment I felt no fear or care in the world let alone the task given to me. I forgot everything about my mother at home and as I looked around I saw my father and my three brothers and felt I was safe from my mother's wrath since most of my family was also enjoying the masquerade parade.

The masquerade band soon moved on to the next village and everyone retreated to their homes, along with my family. I quietly crawled back into the kitchen and continued to wash the butter as if I never left the kitchen. My mother gave me that look. She did not have to say a word, I knew I was in trouble and was all ready to yell for daddy.

To this day, when I am baking at Christmas, especially when I am using butter, my head gets filled with memories of that day. Here's to memories!

SATURDAY NIGHT AT THE SEA WALL

Sea walls are as Guyanese as Guyanese could be. Every Guyanese or visitors to Guyana who has been to our beloved sea wall would have a story and most of the time it would be a very happy story, unless perhaps they had an unfortunate experience. You have never felt a breeze so perfect in temperature bathing your face and gently massaging your entire being. So unique is this sea breeze that not even the mosquitoes are willing to challenge the strength of the salt air coming off the Atlantic Ocean.

I was home recently on a holiday with my family. I was so thrilled I could have my daughter, who is a Canadian, share in some of my fondest memories of my childhood and somehow a new understanding grew between us. It was like all of a sudden she could relate to me and got to know me all over again. She now had a feeling for my life as a child growing up in Guyana and to my surprise she just loved Guyana and has a better appreciation for the simplicity and uncomplicated way of life.

One evening my brother suggested that the family go to the sea wall, I was thrilled. Even as a child the sea wall was always my favorite spot to spend a leisurely evening. As newlyweds, my husband and I spent many, many Saturday evenings relaxing by the Atlantic Ocean. I was so excited that my daughter was about to experience the 'sea wall experience' as fondly called by Guyanese.

I started to tell my daughter, in a childlike excited voice, about my memories of the beautiful sea wall and my evening hangouts; my daughter became as excited and soon became my captive audience.

The sea wall was built by the Dutch when Guyana was under the Dutch occupation, as a wall to keep out the flood waters from the Atlantic Ocean that would often overflow the banks. Parts of Guyana are below sea level and most of the land where the sea wall now stands was all swamp land and would often flood during high tide. The Dutch were the most skillful at irrigation and draining lands. The sea wall was put in place by the Dutch and built manually by the hands of the African slaves. The wall stretched from Georgetown to the East Coast and still stands there to this day as a reminder of slavery and the Dutch occupation while still serving an important purpose of keeping out the flood waters.

Some parts of the wall are very wide and there are park benches to sit on. As you stand on the wall, the warm wind of the Atlantic Ocean can be felt bathing and gently massaging your body with its cool air. The air is so soothing that lovers love to hang out there and I am sure many a love quarrel was settled on that wall. As a matter of fact, the wind is so soothing, it seemed as if you lost all your cares and fell in love all over again with nature.

Families would go there with their young and the children would run and play all kind of games, children playing ketcha (hide and seek) and some playing cowboys and Indians in the semi darkness. Another group would be riding their tricycles and their bicycles while some little girls would be playing hop scotch, marking the bases with white chalk so they can see the bases for jumping in. Then there would be others playing rounders, cricket, dog and the bone, Sal dar, Jumbie, littee (jacks) and bun house. There would be others skipping with two children turning the ropes.

Ketcha and cowboys and Indians were different from the game of hide and seek. The hop scotch game was a large rectangle drawn on the concrete with chalk and the bases would be marked in smaller squares and circles. The player would be given a small chip, like a disk, and the object of the game was to move the disk through the rectangle with all the bases on one foot without stepping on the white lines.

Rounders is a game that is a cross between baseball and cricket played by women and girls. Dog in the bone is where the bone would be hidden by one player and the other would have to find it. The person that finds the bone gets to hide the bone the next time for the other to find.

Sal-dar was a game of two groups facing each other and between the two groups there would be four or five chalk lines drawn on the ground parallel to each other. One person on each side would take turns running across the line while the other person would be in pursuit. The object of the game would be to not get caught or touched by the opponent.

Jumbie was another form of hide and seek with one person being the jumbie and hiding. The object was to find the jumbie and whoever found the jumbie got to be the next jumbie.

Bun house was a game like a puzzle of sorts. An object, such as a rubber ball, would be hidden by one group. The others would have to find the object. The opposite side would give clues such as if you are far from the object, they will shout "water", as you get closer they would shout "smoke" and as you are near the object they would shout "fire". At this point the intensity would build and they would search feverishly for the object.

Living in a poor country, children found ways to have fun in more creative ways than you could ever dream of. All these games were made up by other natives and passed down. I could not help noticing that all the games were games that were a group activity. The children always played in big groups in the evening, after school while supper was being made. After supper they all had to stay in and do their homework.

The laughter of the children warmed your heart and made you smile and filled you with that warm fuzzy feeling. It was always a pleasure to watch the two and three years old trying out their track skills. It was a joy breathing in the fresh salty air, with a hint of a fishy smell, yet not offensive. As a child I enjoyed the gentle massage of the breeze on my face and would turn around in circles until I would get dizzy, fall to the ground and would get up and do it all over again.

The beautiful memories of a moonlit night, looking out at the Atlantic Ocean and seeing the moonlight shinning and shimmering on the rippling waves under the shadow of the moonlight. The sound of the waves hitting against the shoreline making little splashes against the rock beds as if it the water was kissing the rocks. I could still see in my mind's eye lovers holding hands and walking the shoreline in bare feet on the sandy beach and sneaking kisses in the dark.

In one corner of the wall would be vendors with their lanterns lighting their stalls. The lanterns not only shone their light on the items for sale but it also helped the vendors to be seen by all.

There would be the ice cream man on his bicycle, the woman vendor and her hot roasted peanuts, another with her black pudding and souse and yet another with her sugar cakes, pine tarts, Salara, black cake and cassava pone. There would also be the man with his glass case full of Phulouries, Potato balls, Bara, Channa, Egg balls and Plantain chips.

Then on the south side of the wall there was a bandstand. The local steel band and musicians would play for the visitors. This was the time when the local bands practiced their calypso singing. I remember the sound of the Steel Band and the amateurs singing calypso songs. I fondly recall the band having their audience sitting on the grass clapping and cheering along. As I listened and sang, even my heart sang and for a brief moment I would forget all the cares of the world and would be so relaxed, I would get lost in the moment. Some even got up and had a dance or two.

This, my dear daughter, is the sea wall and it truly is a magical place for the natives. It truly gives meaning to the phrase, "No problem man!"

THE BELL RINGER

In the stillness of the day a bell rings in the distance, interrupting the quiet of the day and at the end is a man shouting a very important message. Every child knew they had to be quiet when they heard that bell because it was very important that their parents heard the message being given.

The bell ringer was a culture that was brought to Guyana by the indentured labourer. With the absence of radio and television, it was the people's way of making announcements and spreading news of importance. This was a job that was given only to someone belonging to a certain cast of people known as the Nowah cast. The job of this cast was to be news bearers.

Weddings in Guyana were very different from the more formal type of North American weddings; they were a more open style.

The bell ringer, or Nawaa, would be given full instructions to go around the entire village to each and everyone and extend an invitation to the upcoming celebrations. So, for those who wished to attend, they could do so without confirming a reservation. The food would be cooked all day and guests were fed as they arrived. There were usually two receptions held, one reception at the bride's parent's home and another at the groom's parent's home.

I believe this custom was brought to Guyana by the indentured labourers, because in India the groom would have to travel a far distance to the bride's residence. The bride's home is where the wedding actually took place, so you could see all the excitement and hype at her home. This all happened in the earlier part of the day because after the wedding the bride would travel to the groom's home. Later when the bride and groom arrived at the groom's home, the buzz and excitement would start. The celebration kept going at both residences.

The bell ringer would also inform all the villagers and nearby villagers about the death of someone in the village who may have passed away during the night. The bell ringer would announce the day and time of the funeral, also where the funeral was being held. This custom still goes on today. As a child, whenever you would hear the bell ringer you just knew you had better be quiet so your parents could hear what was being said by the bell ringer.

Another thing that is still a big part of the culture is all of the villagers made a special effort to attend all funerals as they have no excuse about not knowing about the death. As a result of this bell ringer culture, all of the announced invitations were well attended.

The bell ringer would also announce any religious ceremonies that were taking place in the village or nearby villages. For example, a Jagg, which was usually a three, five or seven day event. Jagg was a religious event where thanks would be given in the form of poojahs and a meal would be offered. The event runs all day for several days. Everyone would be invited, yes even children, and they would be sure to have a vegetarian meal and some parsaad (dessert).

The bell ringer, or Nawaa, would also announce if someone was having a Poojah, a dead work (a religious ceremony done by the Hindus after some one died.) The religious function would be on the third day, tenth day or thirteen day or even a one year memorial. Again, all those that were in attendance would be sure to have a vegetarian meal. The meal consisted of rice, Dhal, Bhagee, Pumpkin, potatoes, Katahar, eggplant, cabbage and curried Mango. The culture required that there be seven curries.

There was also a very rare occasion when the bell ringer came out in the dead of night to make an announcement. It would be on a night that the moon would be in eclipse. He would ring his bell and say, "The moon a garahan a laaghaa" which meant the moon is in eclipse.

This announcement would also be used as a warning to all pregnant women not to use a knife of any kind. The people believed that a pregnant woman using a knife during this time would have an adverse effect on the unborn child.

My Aunt Doreen told me a story of two women in the village who were helping out at a wedding one night. The women were using a knife peeling vegetables for the next day, unbeknownst to anyone that the moon was in eclipse. The two women had their babies and both babies were born with cut lips. Everyone was sure the cause of the cut lips was because both women were using knives on the night when the moon was in eclipse.

This was the story of the bell ringer, the invitation that was far more effective than the modern printed version. I guess the point is the old ways were just as effective as the modern way.

It sure lends new meaning to, "the more you change things, the more they remain the same."

THE BOX HAND

In the absence of banks and transportation, the poor people in Guyana found creative ways of saving their money and, better still, quick ways of coming up with fast cash. You would be very surprised to hear someone say they have no money to make a purchase and within a couple of weeks they were able to make the big purchase. When I mention no transportation I meant that the banks were in the city and it meant taking public transportation to get there, which was also costly.

Mr. Johnnie and his wife Suzie lived in a small village about fifty miles from the city of Georgetown, the capital of Guyana. They had seven children and so Suzie stayed home and took care of the children while her husband worked to provide for the family. This couple was so poor they were very hard pressed to make any compulsory savings. For Suzie to be able to be a part of this box hand or partner it meant she would have to make many sacrifices, such as planting her own vegetables for the family consumption. Johnnie would have to fish on the weekends to provide protein for his family.

Mr. Johnnie's motorcycle died and was beyond repair. It was old and worn out and he knew it, but he did not want to admit it. The realization soon hit him and, in a somber voice, he said, "Lord this mean I have to tek the bus to wuk, I can't do that, it gon tek me too long to get to wuk! Lord knows the bus is so slow!" Finally he had to admit it and talk to his wife about the need for another motorcycle. Johnnie said to his wife Suzie, "well gal the old motorbike finally die, dead! Dead! Caput! Done!" Suzie wondered out loud, "Lordie, Lordie, what you gon use fuh wuk, especially with all the late overtime wuk you get?" Johnnie replied to Suzie, "well gal I gon leave that up to you. All I need is some sort of transpote."

Suzie thought of her dilemma and how expensive it would be for John to use public transportation. Even worse still, her husband would not be able to accept overtime work because he would have no way of getting home at night. The public transportation to their village made it last runs at 9 p.m. Suzie cried out loud, "lord, what I will do this hard, hard guava season?" Suzie was thinking so much about her dilemma she got a headache and was unable to sleep that night.

The following morning Suzie decided there had to be a way out to solve the problem. Suzie left home in a hurry and went to see Miss Savebatt, one of her trusted neighbours, to discuss her problem and hope she would help her solve her financial woes.

Suzie pleaded to Miss Savebatt, "I need money as fast as passable, Johnnie need some sort of transpote quick, quick, quick."

Miss Savebatt told Suzie to go home and she would get back to her by the afternoon if she could do anything to help her out. Mrs. Savebatt was one of the elders of the village. Everyone looked up at her as a mother figure and a very trustworthy person. Whenever there is a box hand or partner she would be the person that would oversee the money and its division. She was very well loved.

Miss Savebatt visited some of her neighbours and friends to inquire if they were interested in a box hand (partner). Miss Savebatt told everyone that the box hand or partner would run for twenty weeks and at ten dollars a week each person. In no time at all Miss Savebatt had fifteen neighbours who were interested, five of those people would double their hand to twenty dollars.

This is how the box hand or partner works... twenty people get together to pool ten dollars a week for twenty weeks. This meant that at the end of the twenty weeks they would have saved two hundred dollars. So each week two hundred dollars would be collected and one member of the partnership will receive their portion but will continue to pay their ten dollars each week until the end of the twenty weeks. The person that receives the last hand of two hundred dollars will receive the first hand the next time around.

In the case of Suzie she collected the last hand in order to receive the first hand the next time around. Suzie would have four hundred dollars in a short time. It was certainly a very quick way of saving money without involving the bank. Miss Savebatt agreed to collect the money from everyone and deliver the hand to the appropriate person. The deal was all participating partners gave their money by Saturday evening and the payout was made on a Sunday afternoon.

Well, Suzie and Johnnie soon had the money to solve their dilemma. By collecting the last two hands and the first two hands she now had eight hundred dollars. Johnnie was able to make a down payment on a brand new motorcycle, and hopefully all their problems would be solved. Johnnie would be able to work more overtime and make extra money. Johnnie was so pleased that he had a reliable means of transportation.

The culture of Box hand or partner was brought to Guyana by the Slaves from Africa and they used it to save money without their slave masters knowing. It is a compulsory savings plan and means of saving quick money. This system was done purely on a trust value system. Everyone in the partnership knew it was extremely important to live up to their expectations of paying their dues each and every week on time.

LOOK OUT 'CANE A BUN'

In Guyana, when someone hollered, "cane a bun, look out!", every woman would rush out her house toward the clothes line in the yard where her freshly washed laundry was hanging. It would be a mad scramble and laundry would be put into hands of every available able body as fast as possible. Next would all the windows would be closed.

Miss Tayla, an elderly grandmother who lived not far from the sugar plantation, got up bright and early and did all her laundry. She was always so proud of her accomplishments. Hanging out on the clothes line were all her finest white linen. She paused to admire the beauty of the linen and how white her laundry was. Hanging was her stiffly starched white shirt, pillow slip, tablecloth and curtains. Miss Tayla thought if she got her washing out of the way in the morning it would be dry by the afternoon and she could do her ironing. Wait till I tell you what happened to those pearly white linens that made Miss Tayla madder than a wet hen

Every six months its harvest time for the sugar cane and without any notice to the surrounding residents, the overseer would give the order to burn the cane fields of sugar cane. When this happened the black soot would fly everywhere and contaminate everything in its path, especially the laundry hanging outdoors to dry. Laundry on the clothes lines was a very common site since the only way to dry the laundry was outdoors by the sunshine.

The reason the cane fields were set on fire were to get rid of all the leaves and most of all the rodents and venomous snakes that take up residents in the fields. This fire caused a lot of black soot and dust to fly everywhere. After the fields were burnt, left behind were the long stalks of sugar cane exposed and this made harvesting a lot easier.

The cane was then cut by the labourers using a cutlass (machete). The cane would then be loaded onto punts that were waiting in the canals. The canals were strategically dug around the cane field just for the purpose of harvesting the sugar cane.

The punts were then hooked up one to another and drawn by means of horses that walked along the road. The canals would lead right into the factory where the processing started.

During this time of the year the teenage boys would swim across the canal and steal the unprocessed cane for eating. It was a most comical sight to see. The boys would swim with one hand while they held the other hand up in the air holding their clothes, making sure the clothes didn't get wet. The boys dare not go home with wet clothes because the parents would know exactly what they had been up to. If the parents found out they would sure to be punished and wet clothes would tell the whole tale without a word being said.

There would always be watchmen or guards to keep an eye on the sugar cane so no one would steal it. Every so often a group of boys would be caught by the watchman or guard and they would confiscate the boy's clothes and send them home naked. The boys would have to explain why they were naked.

One such incident did happen. One day a group of boys were caught by the guard named Cowketcha Nabby. The boys saw him coming toward them but they had nowhere to run. One of the boys called out, "Bannas! Bannas! Look Cowketcha Nabby ah come! Oh skites we done fa today." Cowketcha Nabby knew he was no match for the boys running speed, so he did the next best thing; he seized all the boys' clothes. Cowketcha Nabby dared the boys to come and get their clothes. The boys looked at each other and said "what a dilemma! How abee ga get home?"

The boys decided they would cocharr (sweet talk) Cowketcha Nabby and plea tearfully, "ow uncle Nabby give abee the clothes na, abee ga neva do this again!" After pleading and begging for about an hour Cowketcha Nabby pretended he had something to do, so when he turned his back, he gave the boys the opportunity to get their clothes and run as fast as they could. Needless to say this experience did not stop the boys from helping themselves again.

Back to Miss Tayla and what made her so mad one day. All she heard was, "oh skites Mammie, cane a bun, you white clothes, them all turn black with black dust and soot!".

Miss Tayla ran out the house to salvage what she could of the clothes but it was of no use. They were all black and dirty. Miss Tayla was madder than a wet hen. She quarreled with the pale faced Overseer all day but the only thing was, they were no Overseers around to hear her. I guess we can say Miss Tayla was just venting out loud. Miss Tayla got her anger out and the next day she washed and starched her clothes all over again, still fretting as she washed her clothes and hung them on the line.

I should tell you a little more about the sugarcane. About every five to ten years the cane field is usually rested for a year. The fields would be flooded. All the fish that lived in the canals would spread out into the fields and would find a new breeding ground. The rodents and snakes would also take up residence in the abandon fields. The process would revitalize and enrich the soil for the future replanting. As a child I have heard them refer to this process as "banding." I think it was a shortened word for abandonment.

The fields would be drained after its resting period, ploughed, refortified and then replanted. During the period when the fields were drained, the fish would be left vulnerable. The natives would use this opportunity to catch some fish with the aid of a Sain (a small, handheld, round fish net).

My grandmother fondly tells a story of how one day she went on such a fishing trip. She was a very tiny lady, about four feet ten inches and weighed no more than ninety pounds. She looked for a spot to stand where she could fish without getting too deep in the canal. She found what she thought she was a solid piece of dirt, perched of it and started to fish. My grandmother said she caught a full bucket of sweet water fish and was quite pleased, only she did not look forward to cleaning and preparing the fish.

She was feeling very pleased with herself.

As she fished, she suddenly felt the ground from under her feet moved and she could not understand why. Well as she looked down at her feet she saw she was standing on a curled up small Anaconda. My grandmother was so shocked she said she felt the blood drain from her body and her bladder opened up and she was ready to lay an egg right there. Needless to say my grandmother never went fishing in the swamps again.

This is a small sample of some of the pitfalls of living near a sugar plantation. When one was poor, they never had a choice as to where to live. You took what was available to you. In spite of all the inconveniences, the people never complained. They more or less accepted the way of life. Here's to my childhood memories.

SANITATION BACK THEN

Sanitation sounds like a very caring word, but when ignorance was involved that was a totally different story. Sanitation was often carried out in Guyana but the term 'side effect' was a very alien concept. In an effort to cure one problem it created many others.

I was looking at a show on television about Africa and immediately started to think back on my childhood and the unsanitary conditions around me when I was growing up. I thought of my granddaughter and how fortunate she was that she would never have to experience such awful living conditions. I felt compelled to write about my unsanitary conditions and hope that my granddaughter will learn something from my experience.

At the time I was growing up in Guyana, the British were in control of the country. They used some awful means of sanitation with little regard for the long term effects on human lives, or maybe they themselves were not conscious of the side effects. The sanitation gang is what they were called back then. I remember all the swampy area, like Drains and Ditches, being sprayed with DDT. In my childhood innocence, I was so fascinated by the men spraying I would stand fairly close by the workers and watch them work. The only protection the men had on were long rubber boots. I shiver to think of what all that DDT the workers inhaled and what might have done to them. However the jury is still out on the DDT. It still remains a very controversial subject as to the use or lack of.

The reason for such radical and aggressive measures was the government's way of trying to control the spread of malaria outbreaks. Should there be such an outbreak it would surely tax the health care system, which would be even more costly.

The other thing that happened was as soon as there was confirmation of a Malaria outbreak, workers were sent out to go to every home in the evening. Once the worker is at the house, he took a blood sample on a glass slide and labeled it. I remember well, as the worker was finishing taking the blood samples and putting it in its container, without even washing his hands, he would dispense Quinine tablets to each and everyone.

The fact that someone would be allergic to Quinine was never a consideration or even of any consequence to the workers. Perhaps the worker himself was not informed of the dangers he was dealing with. I remember becoming very ill, nauseous, and sick to my stomach. I vomited non stop for about three days. This all started half hour after the medication was taken. I guess you could say I was definitely allergic to the Quinine.

Malaria means "bad air", formerly called Ague (acute fever) or marsh fever. Malaria is an infectious disease common in many tropical countries. This disease was caused by a parasite of the genus plasmodium that was transmitted primarily by the female anopheles mosquito. The plasmodium parasite invades and consumes the red blood cells of the infected person. The symptoms are fever, shivering, joint pain, vomiting, convulsions, and anemia caused by haemolysis in really severe cases of coma, which can lead to death. It is very important for people in these countries to use a mosquito net to sleep under. It is possible that with the evolutionary pressure of malaria, the human genes can lead to:

1. Sickle Cell
2. Thalassemias
3. Daffy antigens

Young children and pregnant women were very vulnerable.

As a young child I also remember everyone taking their whole family to the local hospital every three months for a dose of castor oil. I am not sure what this was for but I suspect it had to do with parasite-like worms. The only good memory I have of the whole exercise was the orange slices that my mother would give us after the dose of castor oil, to take the taste away.

I recall some children being so terrified of the exercise and would scream and refuse to open their mouths. The adults and nurses would literally hold the child down and while squeezing their nose would pour the castor oil into their mouths. The bottom line was you were given that oil whether you wanted it or not. Documentation would be made of the visit and if any did not show up they would be given a visit from hospital personnel.

SANITATION BACK THEN

I clearly recall being taken to the local hospital when I was sick and was diagnosed by the sick nurse and he would even prescribe medication he saw fit. I am sure many children were misdiagnosed but I do know that when conventional medicine did not work it was back to good old bush remedies or, as we say today, alternative medicine.

I guess I am still very grateful that with all the negatives of the sanitation system at least there was some sanitation. I am still not sure how I really feel about the method of sanitation but in the authority's mind they were doing what they thought was best for all, whether it was a political or humanitarian decision. I would like to think their intentions were pure and good.

WASH DAY

Even in this modern day and time, laundry is still a very time consuming task. Can you imagine for a moment how difficult it would be to do laundry without running water at your disposal? Take a walk down memory lane with me as I tell you how the laundry was done back in the days when I was a child.

I was reflecting one day about how the laundry was done back in the days of my childhood. I was thinking of how labour intensive a task it was because of the lack of water in the homes. I started to reflect on all the changes that have taken place during my lifetime. As I started to do my own laundry, I started to reflect on how laundry was done when I was a child, then I thought I should write about this for my granddaughter, since she would have no clue whatsoever about such difficult times.

As I recall there were two methods of doing the laundry. The method depends on what cultural background the launderer was from, whether you were from an Indian background or an African background.

For the people of an African background, their method of laundering was done by using a large galvanized tub or a half of a wooden barrel. The heavily soiled clothes were placed in the galvanized tub to boil on an open fire to help remove any stubborn stains, with some lye added to the water. The next step was they were hung out in the sun to bleach some more. After a couple of hours the clothes would be picked up and put back in the tub and soaked with soap again.

Then by the means of a scrub board, which was placed in the tub, the clothes were then rubbed on the scrub board to remove any remaining dirt with the help of some lye soap. The scrub board was about thirty inches long and fifteen inches wide with groves or ribs carved into the board. The clothes would be soaped well and vigorously rubbed on the board. The friction of the clothes rubbing against the board would remove the dirt.

Water was always at a premium. It had to be fetched in buckets from an artesian well to the house to do all the chores, including the laundry. This well was usually a fair distance from the home since the whole village used the same well. The other means of water was rain water. Large barrels were placed at the end of the eaves trough to collect the rain water that was drained in a rainfall.

The laundry was first scrubbed in the tub on the scrub board, then it was rinsed thoroughly to remove all soap, all the whites would get a second rinse in blue water. Most of the cottons would be starched and hung to dry. The final stage was the pressing, which was done by a flat iron heated on a wood stove or a coal pot.

The second method was a method brought from India by the indentured labourers. As water was at a prenium, people found inventive ways of coping with their dilemma. The Indians would build a wash stand by the canals, rivers and trenches. The stand was like a platform of sorts about five feet long and four feet wide.

The ladies would sit on a small bench, which was called 'peerha' and, with the aid of a thick wood paddle called a 'beata' (about fifteen inches long, six to eight inches wide and two inches thick and shaped like a paddle), they would beat the clothes on the board with the beata. The beating action helped remove all the dirt from the clothes. Again a half barrel or galvanized pan would be used to soak the clothes in preparation for washing. I guess it would be considered as a pre-wash method.

The soap that was used for washing the laundry was homemade from coconut oil. Today's alternative medicine followers have given this same soap great reviews and recommendations. The method used was the same as a method called castile soap. I believe the method used was a cold press which was made with oil and lye.

The rest of the laundry was done much the same way as the first method. The laundry was blue rinsed and starched much the same way.

The two methods of laundering were different, one more labor intensive than the other but basically the end results were the same, clean clothes. They believed the blue rinse that was used helped to keep the whites looking white.

Even the ironing wasn't an exact science. They had to gauge the right temperature of the flat irons and as the iron cooled off, the more delicate pieces were ironed. The people might have been dirt poor but they looked like a million bucks when they stepped out.

This is my reflection and memory of wash day growing up in Guyana. As I was thinking of the soap and the fact that it contained no strong detergents, I couldn't help but think how we are self destructing with all the chemicals we employ today in the name of quicker and cleaner.

Palm Coconut Soap

24 ounces of coconut oil
64 ounces of palm oil
12 ounces of lye
23 ounces of water
1.6 ounces of fragrance of choice

Method:

This was all mixed, stirred well and poured in moulds.

How the soap is made:

Soap is a mixture of Soda, Potash and fatty acids derived from oil.

The soap was made from the coconut oil and was called castile soap. I believe the method used for making soap was the cold press which was made with oil and lye.

WHAT WILL I FEED THE BABY?

Feeding a baby today is a far cry from the way the babies were fed years ago. There was no such thing as baby formulas, let alone fortified formulas. Yet, in spite of this there were some very brilliant minds in the days of old. Here is my memory of how a baby was fed when I was a child.

Sitting quietly in an office I overheard two young couples complaining of how expensive it was to buy baby formula and disposable diapers for the babies. While I was listening to such a conversation, I lost some of what was being said because my mind and thoughts drifted back to growing up in a poor country and how the poor people fed and took care of their babies.

Then I thought of what I experienced in my childhood and how this experience would now be an alien concept to this young generation. I thought of my own granddaughter and her generation, how difficult it would be for her generation to even fathom the struggles of poor people in third world countries.

I guess you could say that prompted me to write this chapter.

I started to reflect on how fortunate this generation has been with the good fortune of readymade fortified formulas for the babies and even better, disposable diapers. No diapers to wash meant more time to spend with their little ones. There is no doubt this new way is very healthy and best for babies. I am still not sure that the children are any smarter especially since mothers' milk is still the number one choice. The only difference is the mothers of this generation have a choice while back them it was not even a consideration, let alone a choice. My mind, still drifting, thought of how the mothers coped and what the babies were fed.

I know someone is going to say, "what did the mother who did not have enough breast milk do to feed the babies?" Well, the answer I have will really surprise some of the modern generation. The very poor people in such countries have a community kinship among them that goes very deep.

Mothers who had an ample supply of breast milk would volunteer to wet nurse (breast feed) the other babies of their friends. I remember my mother telling me that when I was born she just did not have sufficient milk to satisfy me so a neighbour fed me until she was able to produce enough milk to feed me. My mother-in-law told me she breast fed my husband until he was seven years old. This one did boggle my mind!

So what were these babies fed? The first choice for babies was breast milk. Other choices were goat, sheep or cow's milk. The milk from these animals was sterilized on the wood stove or fireside. The milk was good old fashioned whole milk. I did not know about two percent, one percent or even skim milk until I came to live in North America.

I remember as a child I would steal the thick buttery cream from the top of the sterilized milk and savor every moment of eating that cream. I remember my mother saying, "I have to speak with the milkman. It seems as if he is adding water to this milk, this cream is just not rich or not thick enough these days." Little did she know I was the cream thief.

I remember the creamy taste of food like porridge, custard, fudge and puddings because it was made with whole milk. The full bodied flavour of the fudge just melted in my mouth like nothing I have ever tasted today. I do not remember eating margarine as we didn't have any. It was good old fashion butter.

There is nothing like hot baked bread with real butter on it. Yum! Yum! Yum! Oh so mouth watering.

Then as the children got a bit older they were given porridge or as the Guyanese call it 'pap.' Here are some of the porridges as I remember them, which were made to feed the infant and toddler children at the end of my story.

The nursing bottle was a Coco Cola or Pepsi bottle made of thick glass. Believe me, it was thick, I know because that bottle was thrown across the floor many, many times and never broke. Sometimes it would get the odd little chip. The nipple was a large thick rubber cone shaped with a thick, rolled up rubber brim, which was stretched over the mouth of the bottle. I remember the strength it took to stretch a new nipple over the rim, many a bottle of porridge was spilled trying to put on a new nipple.

Then, there was the day when absolutely nothing was available to feed the baby so lemon grass was boiled and milk added and was used for the baby food. They were also fed plain old green tea or black tea and yes, even coffee. There were times when the milk wasn't affordable or available. I remember times when the baby was given plain old warm water with sugar added. Such is the life of poverty and hard times.

These were the times when a mother's heart cried silently inward.

As the child got older, which was about six months old, they would be given more solid food like mashed eddoes, cassava, rice, plantain with eggs or fish and some mashed fruit that was in season with the most popular choice being banana. Sometimes biscuits or bread would be soaked in milk and fed to the child. I remember the babies being given a teaspoon of cod liver oil every day.

There were those days when none of the above mentioned would be available or money was not available to purchase any of them. It was those times when the choice would be flours or rice porridge.

Flour Porridge: soak a few tablespoon of flour in a generous amount of water and mix well to remove all lumps. The paste was then added to a saucepan of boiling water and brought to a boil. Cinnamon, vanilla essence and nutmeg would be added for flavoring. Then over a slow fire to prevent scorching, the porridge would be brought to a full rolling boil. The porridge would them be removed from the fire and milk added. It was sweetened and then served to baby in the bottle.

Rice porridge: Cook rice until soft in generous amount of water until soft, very soft, like mush. Add spices such as vanilla essence, cinnamon and nutmeg. Add milk and sugar and feed to baby.

Cassava Porridge: Peel, wash and grate cassava. Boil in a generous amount of water until cassava in cooked. Again it would be flavoured with the spices of choice or availability. Generous amounts of milk would be added. It was sweetened and served warm.

Plantain Porridge: Wash and peel plantain, them grate on a fine grater. Boil in generous amount of water with spices of choice. Boil until plantain is well cooked. Add generous amount of milk and strain to remove all lumps. Sweeten and pour warm into a baby's bottle.

Cornmeal Porridge: Corn meal is measured and soaked in cold water. In a saucepan bring water to a boil adding flavouring of choice. Add cornmeal to boiling water and allow to thicken. Add milk and sugar and serve warm.

Sago or Tapioca Porridge: Measure and soak sago in cold water, allowing enough time for sago to hydrate. In a saucepan bring water to a boil and add your flavouring of choice and sago. Stir constantly to prevent scorching. Boil until buds are transparent. Add milk and sweeten, serve warm to baby.

Barley Pap: Wash and boil barley in a generous amount of water. As the barley grain boils, it will thicken. The liquid is then drained leaving the barley grain to be eaten. Milk would be added to the barley water along with sugar. Then poured in the baby's bottle and served.

This is how I remember my mother coping with a new baby in the home during those difficult financial times or as Guyanese would say "hard times."

ABOUT THE AUTHOR

I was born in Guyana and moved to Canada thirty-four years ago with my husband Rolly. I have three children... my late son Andrew, second son Terry and my daughter Cindy, and their spouses. Because of the busy lifestyle I lived while my own children were young, I neglected to pass on some childhood stories, told to me by my mother on a starry moonlight night on the front porch. These stories were told to us on Friday or Saturday nights when my father was working the evening shift. They bring back fond memories of my childhood and the evening snacks of freshly made plantain chips, fresh hot roasted peanuts, ice cold mauby and cream soda mixed with carnation milk with lots of ice.

When my granddaughter was born, as I held her and gazed into her beautiful brown eyes, I felt so humble and yet so blessed and privileged to be the grandmother of this beautiful gift. I looked at my own daughter Cindy and I asked, "what kind of a legacy do I have to pass on to this angel God has given me?" My so very wise daughter said "Mom, write your grandchild the stories you have always wanted to write, give her a glimpse into your childhood and she will also have them to pass on in later years."

Well I thought about my daughter's suggestion and the more I thought, the more motivated I became. My wonderful husband of thirty eight years got me a laptop and said "here you go, start writing; I am here for you if you need me." I thought of the fact that there might be a lot of grandmothers out there who can relate to my story and so I sat at my laptop and this book was born.

I have written this book for all the grandparents and parents to read to their little ones, and don't neglect to pass on their legacy; it is truly beautiful and rich. I plan to read to my grandchildren every chance I get.

Norma

www.ingramcontent.com/pod-product-compliance
Lightning Source LLC
Chambersburg PA
CBHW080251170426
43192CB00014BA/2635